I0481137

The Donkey of

Financial

Education

Introduction

Financial education is very important for making financially informed decisions. The person who is bad in terms of financial education makes poor spending decisions and wastes his Money in extravagant activities, and he has poor knowledge about finances that is why he is given the title of the donkey of financial education. This book enlightens the readers about key concepts such as financial education, the importance of financial education, the role of money management for the purpose of saving, investing, spending, and earning. It then explains the concept of financial education by giving examples of three types of people who belong to three different categories of financial education. The person who is poorer in terms of saving and investing is termed as the donkey of financial education, whereas a person who makes illogical decisions although he tries to save but do not get successful in saving enough Money gets a C grade, which means he has been awarded this grade because of unsatisfactory performance in the financial report card. On the other hand, a person who is efficient in financial performance gets an A+ grade and is awarded excellent remarks because of his efficient financial management skills.

This e-book also explores the example of an employee who ends up wasting his hard-earned salary due to his bad and inefficient financial planning and becomes a perfect example of a donkey of financial education. He ends up in negative debt as he makes reckless financial decisions. In contrast, an employer takes benefit of the donkey behavior of his employees and avoids recruiting new members in his office. He then invests the profit obtained due to extra time given by this employee in a productive and innovative venture, which increases the value of his Money. In short, this book is an explanation of the need to invest in financial education and compels readers to wake up before it is too late as it is the need of the hour to enhance their knowledge of financial education and efficient money management. And in the end, the key to success is discussed, which is the concept of frugality, which can be achieved through cutting back of one's expenses. In this way, a person will be able to initiate a personal change in the habits of the donkey of financial education.

Table of Contents

Chapter 1: What is financial education?

Financial education can be defined as the capability to get an understanding of how Money works. It is the skill that involves how to invest and manage Money in an improved way and how to make better financial decisions. Millions of people around the world make financial decisions, and their consequences are unbearable. People involved are crooked life insurance agents and other financial service providers who misguide the financially uneducated person out of the Money earned through honest means by endorsing financial goods that are not beneficial for them and hiding relevant information. There is a widespread term to describe this, which is named miss-selling. People lose money by making bad financial decisions and end up utilizing Money they had saved for years. They acquire loans without understanding interest payments and the repercussions of default. People may resort to committing suicide if they are facing financial trouble and no because they are not well health-wise. If you lack financial education, you will end up having saved nothing for retirement as you had already spent your money on needless expenses. If you have no financial education, it will be a heavy drain on the Nation's resources as expenditure to meet financial security rise. This takes us to the question that How can we enhance the financial literacy of a nation as a whole and accomplish far-reaching financial inclusion?

The answer lies in developing awareness regarding financial education across society.

Understanding the concept of Financial Learning

In recent years, the concept of financial goods and services has become increasingly prevalent across the whole society. The people of earlier generations of Americans might have the habit of purchasing goods primarily in cash, but today, many credit products are common, like the use of credit cards, bank loans, and student loans. Other services like health insurance and self-guided investment accounts have also gained popularity. This has made it even more vital for individuals to develop an understanding of how to use them in a responsible manner. Although there are a large number of techniques that may fall under the ambit of financial literacy, the examples of which include a household budget, understanding how to efficiently manage and pay back a mortgage, and weighing the adjustments between different credit and investment services. Oftentimes, this expertise requires adequate knowledge of key economic terms, such as composite interest and the worth of money with time. Given the significance of finance in the modern world, the dearth of financial literacy can be very detrimental to the long-term financial success of a person. There is a lack of finances in many countries, including the United States, where according to estimates of the Financial Industry Regulatory Authority (FINRA), not less than 66% of Americans lack financial literacy.

The absence of financial literacy can lead to a number of difficulties. First of all, financially uneducated individuals may be more prone to gather unmanageable debt burdens, for instance, through poor outlay decisions or through a lack of long-term groundwork. This has the tendency to make a person poor in terms of credit, bankrupt, lead to housing foreclosure, or other negative concerns. Appreciatively, there are now various institutions available for those who are aspiring to educate themselves about the financial world.

Financial literacy; a stepping stone for financial inclusion:

Now the next big item is how financial education can be a first step in obtaining financial inclusion. Financial inclusion allows access to financial services like banking and insurance for all citizens at a reasonable cost. A financially learned person knows the significance of financial inclusion, and this is the first stage of financial inclusion.

- Financial inclusion insists on the formation of a bank account for saving and investing. A person who is fiscally educated understands this and will acquire a savings bank account to attain the benefits related to live indemnification and personal accident insurance to save him from avaricious money lenders.
- Financial education emboldens citizens to get rid of the informal

financial system operated by greedy money lenders and illegal funds to come to the formal financial system, which involves banks and insurance.

- Financial education is equally beneficial and valuable as the concept of financial inclusion. People will learn to save, invest, borrow and spend intelligently. A person who is financially educated won't ask why we need financial inclusion but drives it. This solves all problems related to financial inclusion. When there is financial inclusion, rural citizens will feel empowered, will protect themselves from financial scams, and adopt online transaction methods like mobile payment systems, making the Government's role in financial inclusion really minimal.

The best way to achieve financial education is by teaching young minds at the school level. It can be attained by making some changes in the education curriculum. Children must be familiarized with financial literacy at the school level to both rural and inner-city students, and presently, financial concepts are not given, even at the degree level.

- One big way of accomplishing financial literacy is enlightening the girl child. If financial education is given at a young age, it empowers women in later stages of our society. They, in turn, teach their kids to save and invest, contributing to a developed Nation.
- There's a widespread belief that the rich tend to be more financially literate. It is not correct. Financial literacy is equally important for all citizens and especially for the rich financially illiterate citizens, to save and protect wealth.
- It's the duty and obligation of every person to make himself financially literate by taking financial literacy into their own hands. Information is vital to financial literacy, and nothing is more important than evaluating your personal finance. The next step would be to understand your finances and making the correct decisions related to your finance.
- Introducing a practical style to seek financial literacy in order to promote financial inclusion. Researches have demonstrated that financial literacy programs where service suppliers were involved and supported by a

suitable financial product. It motivates citizens to use that product. Citizens will use that financial services if they feel that it is according to their requirements.

- Banks could also impart financial education to leaders of remote communities, and this information would permeate to the lowest segments of society, reaching every citizen in the country.
- Financial services that cater to the needs of low-income people must be announced, and a financial education provided to inspire citizens to use these products, and they will be able to involve in the formal financial sector and enjoy financial prosperity.

Therefore, we can say that financial literacy is a process to understand and effectively utilize various financial expertise, including personal money management and investment. The lack of this expertise is named financial illiteracy. A strong basis of financial literacy could help in fulfilling various life goals, like saving for education or retiring on time, by means of debt responsibly, and organizing a business.

Formulating a strategy for financial literacy in order to increase your personal finances involves learning and performing a variety of skills linked to the budget, managing, and paying back debts. These are some of the practical strategies to consider:

Creating a budget:

It includes tracking the amount of cash you receive on a monthly basis in comparison to how much you devote in an excel sheet, on paper, or to an app designing for budgeting. Your budget should involve income, for instance, information about paychecks, investments, allowance, fixed expenditures like rent of the house, services, payments of loans, luxuries like eating out, shopping, and travel expenses related to recreation and savings.

Making a payment to yourself first

It can be done by building savings, and this inverse budgeting strategy includes selecting a savings goal like a down payment for a home and then determining how much you want to donate toward it each month, and saving that amount before you distribute the rest of your expenditures.

Managing your bill payment

In order to stay on top of bills on a monthly basis so that payments steadily arrive on time. Consider taking benefit of automatic withdrawals from a checking account or bill-paying apps, and sign up for email, phone, or mail payment reminders.

Get your credit report

For once in a year, consumers can get a free credit report from the major credit bureaus like Transunion. Evaluate it, and any errors can be disputed by notifying the credit bureau of inaccuracies.

Check your credit score:

If you have a good credit score, it helps in obtaining the best interest rates on credits and credit cards other than benefits. You can Monitor your score with a free credit monitoring service (and if you have access and want to add an additional layer of protection on your information) and get to know of the financial choices that can increase or lower your score, like credit inquiries and operation rates.

Managing debt

Suppose you utilize your budget to stay on top of debt through reduction of spending and increasing reimbursement. Make a reduction plan for debt, such as payment of loan with highest interest rate. If your debt is too much, then contact creditors to renegotiate payment, acquire loans, or discover a debt-counseling program.

Investing in the future:

If your employer is offering a 401(k) retirement savings account, make sure to make it operational and contribute the maximum to collect the employer benefit. You can open an IRA and create an expanded investment portfolio of stocks, fixated revenue, and commodities. You need to seek financial guidance from professional advisors for the purpose of determining how much amount you will need to live retirement life comfortably and to make strategies to reach your goal.

Need of Financial Literacy:

Subjects like financial management may not be especially beneficial to learners during their high school years; they will prove valuable throughout the next years of their lives. Understanding notions such as interest rates, opportunity related costs, debt administration, compound interest, and budgeting, for example, could greatly help students in managing the student loans so that they may rely on funding their tuition fee and keeping them from amass precarious levels of debt and threatening their credit scores. Similarly, the topics like income taxes and retirement planning will ultimately prove useful for all students, no matter what they do after high school. The low level of financial education, the antagonistic effects that it develops on financial behavior, and the susceptibilities of certain clusters throw light on the need and importance of financial schooling. Financial education is a strong foundation in order to raise financial literacy and inform the next groups of consumers, employees, and citizens. Many countries have made efforts in recent years to work towards this endeavor and provide financial literacy in schools, colleges, and places of work. However, the constantly low numbers of financial literacy across the world specify that a piece of the riddle is not there. When it comes to providing financial knowledge, one principle cannot be applied to all. Other than that, in order to have the potential for a large-scale operation, the main mechanism for any financial literacy program should be good content that is restricted to specific audiences. An operative financial education program resourcefully recognizes the needs of its audience, precisely targets susceptible groups, has clear goals, and relies on demanding evaluation metrics.

Reasons for financial education:

There are three persuasive reasons to have financial education in school. First, if you expose young people to the basic concepts involved in financial decision-making, you will be imparting them the skill to make valuable and consequential fiscal decisions.

Secondly, schools build connections of financial literacy with groups who may not be aware of it and may not get the chance, for instance, females. Third, it is imperative to decrease the costs of acquiring financial literacy if we want to get access to higher financial literacy both among people and among society. There are many reasons to have personal finance courses at the college level as well. In the same way in which colleges and universities offer sequence in company finance to learn how to accomplish the finances of firms, so it is need of students to acquire the knowledge for the purpose of managing their own savings over the lifetime. Finally, it is important to offer financial literacy in the community, in spaces where people go to acquire knowledge.

Financial education is very important for making financially intelligent and informed decision making. Hundreds of thousands of people residing around the world are not learning the art of making financial decisions, and they have to face grave consequences in the form of loss of money, and they end up with no money for their retirement life. There are life insurance agents and other financial service providers whose job is to guide the financially uneducated person so that they save an efficient amount of Money by managing their expenses. Only then will they be able to learn the art of budget-making in which they make a list of items that they need on a daily basis and are essential. The learning of financial education is especially important for poor people; otherwise, they will lose their hard-earned money by making bad financial decisions and end up using Money they had saved for years. They need to acquire loans with a full understanding of interest payments and the consequences in case they default. People might resort to unthinkable endeavors if they are in financial difficulty and no because they are not unwell, generally. So we can say that if a person lacks financial education, he will end up having saved nothing for retirement as he had already spent his money on needless expenses. The importance of financial education cannot be overemphasized from the fact that financially illiterate people are a heavy drain on the resources of a state, as that nation can never achieve the state of financial inclusion.

Chapter 2: Introduction to money management

What Is Money Management?

Money management is related to the processes, which include the formation of a budget, ways to save money, how to invest money, spending, or else administration of the capital of an individual or group. The leading use of the phrase in financial education is through investing in specialized decision-making for investment for a large number of funds, such as joint funds or pension plans. A family budget is vital to the management of your Money. Money management broadly referred to the processes that are exploited to record and manage the finances of an individual, household, or organization. Financial consultants and personal finance stages like mobile apps are all the time more common in helping individuals manage their money in an efficient manner. If you manage Money badly, it can lead to cycles of liability and financial strain. But the dilemma is we are not taught tactics of financial management from the start in educations. We only learn it through the traditional family concept of saving, spending, and earning. That's why we are not familiar with specialized methods of saving and spending Money.

The most traditional concept taught to us by the family of saving, spending, and investing are:

- spending your Money astutely on the things you must have and prioritize what are your needs
- saving Money for the stuff you like to have but can live without, and minimize what your wants are
- Setting aside Money for unanticipated expenses. For example, if your vehicle breaks down and needs maintenance.
- Take a break to avoid occasional overspending.

Then family budget includes setting aside money that you require for everyday essentials like household expenses as food, mortgage, utility expenses like gas, electricity, internet bill, education, transport, and medical services in order to help you make sure that you have enough money saved for unpredictable expenses and crises.

In contrast, Money management gives you knowledge about the management of investment and management of the portfolio.

The Basics of Money Management

Money management is an extensive term that contains and combines services and resolutions that encompass the whole investment industry. In the market, consumers have access to a wide range of assets and claims that make them manage at the individual level and cover nearly every domain of their personal savings. As investors increase the net value of their investment, they often seek the facilities of financial advisors for proficient money management. Financial advisors are classically associated with private banking-related services, which offers maintenance for all-inclusive money management plans that can involve property planning, retirement, and more. Money management is the process of tracking expenses, investment planning, budget making, banking, and evaluation of taxation of Money.

Money management is a tactical method to make Money produce the highest interest and output value for any quantity of money spent. Spend Money to fulfill longings (irrespective of whether they can rightly be included in a budget) is a natural human desire. The idea of management techniques has been established to reduce the quantity of cash that persons, companies, and institutions spend on items that had added no substantial value to their standards of living, long-term assortments, and assets. Warren Buffett, in one of his biographies, cautioned prospective investors to experiment with his highly esteemed "frugality" ideology. This involves making every financial transaction meaningfully:

1. Avoiding any expense that pleas to vanity or snobbery
2. Always go for the most profitable alternative (for instance, establishing a small quality and varied yardsticks, if any)
3. Preferring expenditures on interest-bearing items over other items.
4. Establishing the probable benefits of every anticipated expenditure using the canon of plus/minus/nil to the standard of quick value system.

These practices are for a boost of investment and multiplication of portfolio. There are various companies as well that offers facilities, providing help and different models for the management of Money. These are intended to manage grace assets and making them grow. Investment money management is also a crucial dimension of the investment industry overall. Investment company money management provides individual customers investment funding options that contain all investable asset classes in the monetary market. Investment company money managers also important for the sustenance of the capital management of official clients, with investment solutions for institutional retirement planning, endowments, basics, and more.

What is portfolio management?

Stock portfolio management can either be inactive or active. Inert portfolios prefer making an investment in ETFs and mutual funds to follow certain directories. Dynamic portfolios can be managed by management teams with specific strategies. The management of a debt portfolio usually contemplates risk of credit, risk of interest rate, and last but not least risk of reinvestment. Other investments can further expand a collection and lower the methodical risk. Examples of substitute investments include private equities, undertaking capitals, supplies, and real estate. Portfolio and management of investment can be very complicated and necessitates expertise. Professional money managers apply multiple schemes efficiently and in an effective manner to reach a higher expected return at the given level of danger. Investment risk is directly proportional to the return in a well-organized portfolio. The main idea of money management is to create an equilibrium between the risk and return to maximize the utility of investors.

Methods of making a fruitful investment:

Getting a Health-Savings-Account

For a less-exotic but still progressive idea, you should consider initiating a Health-Savings-Account (HSA). An HSA is an account accessible to individuals or families with high-deduction health policies. They will propose tax benefits, like allowing charities to be deducted on your taxes. Your investment then will sit and grow tax-free until you extract it to cover a qualified health-care expense. But probably the best part is that once you turn more than sixty, the savings can be reserved penalty-free for any motive. There are restrictions, and you can only invest a certain amount of money in an HSA, as said and suggested by your deductible and your family condition. But even if you're only allowed to make an uncertain contribution, the tax benefits are always worth your effort.

People-to-People Lending

Another policy to consider if you only have a certain amount to invest in is peer-to-peer lending platforms. Loaning Club is one of the biggest, and as an investor, you have the option to spread your investments over hundreds or thousands of loans in increments as low as twenty-five dollars. You only need thousands of dollars to get started, and you can mechanize your investments based on your criteria prior to selection.

Bank Account Bonus investment

While Bank of America is full thinking up new dues for the purpose of charging its customers, there are other banks too that are still giving large bonuses to new customers where they open an account. Bank bonuses are one of the fastest ways to earn money and can yield a substantial return on your money in a short amount of time.

Horse Breeding

If you do not have the income to invest in a full-blown stud farm, but even if you have of the amount in the range of hundreds of dollars, you can make a moderate investment, and it can still make a profit by horse-ownership. With an extraordinary cost of entry and above-average risks, ownership-partnerships are a prevalent means of dispersal of the expense, and there are no risks of racehorse ownership. You're essentially crowd-sourced a racehorse. Investing in a horse is by no means guarantees a return. But with prize purses progressively increasing over more than a few years, the possible returns can be huge. So for the investor who is fond of taking some chances, becoming a partner on a horse can be one of the more thrilling options.

Online Real Estate Investment

They often remind us that land is the only thing that enhances the value of Money, and its importance certainly reflects that. But in spite of the high return potential, not everyone has the revenues or inclination to be a landlord. But similar to horse-raising, there is an explanation. Services like Fund rise have cracked, which motivates small investors to come together to invest in isolated real-estate holdings. And the most important thing is that you never have to make any considerable effort to do any building maintenance. The services themselves hold that for a minimal fee.

Investment in Fine Wine business

For the investor who is fond of having the finer things in life, wine can hold a personal appeal to some extent. It can also hold noteworthy economic appeal. The value of fine wine increases substantially as it grows up, and can reach new highs by as much as one-third of the original prize, once it's labeled as investment-grade. Steadfast vintages are even followed on an index of fine wines, so you can follow them just like a stock of blue-chip.

Automated Gold Investing

Much like other investment ideas discussed above, gold and valuable metals are commodities that carry intrinsic value. And the added advantage of making an investment in these metals is that they are predominantly valued in times of economic distress.

Think Outside Stocks and Bonds for Resourceful Investments

If you make an investment repetitively, you are destined to succeed because it is one of the greatest ways to prepare for your future. Especially in the case that when your future becomes harder to forecast every day and you always think that you have terrible things waiting for you. A major portion of your investment strategy should be devoted to seeking inventive and resourceful investments. Beyond often coming with unconventional perks of their own, they are a great way to help protect your business and yourself from uncertainty. If you have financial goals like saving for the future (in the case of retirement), it will also help you in fulfilling this goal.

Money management is related to the process of pursuing and forecasting on use of capital of an individual or an individual. In personal finance, money management involves the process of budgeting, spending meaningfully, saving a large sum, and investing in productive and resourceful ventures. In business finance, management of Money covers the nurture and use of capital. The budget of the firm is mainly prejudiced by its business policies. In fiscal markets, money management refers to the management of portfolio and savings management.

Chapter 3: Financial education report card of the person with poor and excellent financial education

Financial report card:

A personal financial statement, also named a financial report card, will deliver all the essential information needed to decide whether a person is creditworthy or not. It is said that a person's financial statement is their report card in school because it offers more information about a person than any other personal documents about the financial life of that person.

A person's financial statement educates you about:

- One's priorities in spending and investment,
- One's spending behaviors
- His investments
- And whether he has a great future and saved enough or not.

Definition of financial statement?

A basic financial statement is a mixture of two documents, which are an income statement and a balance sheet. A sample financial statement is composed of 5 main components.

Income: which is the Money you earn.

Expenses: total Money spent on needs of daily life

Assets: a thing that helps you in earning and adds Money to your pocket

Liabilities: a thing that deprives you of Money.

Cash flow: it is obtained by subtraction of Income and expenses

These five things complete a life report card of a person and can tell a lot about the story of somebody's life.

Poor/ Middle-class and Rich report card:

The poor and middle class have limited sources of income like their job. Therefore, they make use of their salaries to meet their expenses and buy obligations. They do not have many properties. The rich, on the other hand, possess properties that generate a passive income that they use to cover their expenditures and problems. The poor and middle-class lives will be ruined if they lose job contract, whereas the rich possess a large number of assets and will have enough money for their needs almost forever.

Donkey of financial education

A donkey of financial education is a person who always spends his Money without thinking much and therefore ends up in debt. That's why he always comes last, as children with bad academic results come last. He is not aware of the concept of financial frugality and therefore spends Money in overzealous manner and, like a bad student, doesn't care much about his study and is not aware of the fact that his prosperous future is linked to his good academic performance. In the same vein, the donkey of financial education is a gullible person who is financially illiterate, uneducated, and unaware of the concept of financial management. He is spending money on frivolous things without caution and in an imprudent way, which makes him stupid and financially illiterate. He will get an 'F' because he has failed in the management of his finances. If there are financial report card issued by the school to evaluate his financial performance, he will get a low grade, which is C to give him the awareness that he should wake up before he ends up in more and more chaos as he is not saving much for his and his family's future.

Given below are some of the indicators to say that this person encompasses certain habits, because of which he is given the title of the donkey of financial education.

Not keeping a budget

When a donkey of financial education spends his Money without investing and saving, at some point, people ask him where is all his money going? He realizes that forming a budget isn't a funny thing, but it's essential for your financial safety. It would have helped him manage his expenses, so he would know exactly how much he had been earning and how much he had been spending, and how. The truth is, he should have noted his expenses how much he should be spending money on food, clothing, coffee, and other essentials. All these are expenses that he should have tracked. Now, he has found himself with too much month at the end of his salary.

Paying bills late

He is also in the habit of paying bills after their due date. It might be utility bills, electricity bills, and any other kind of bills for that difficulty. He had waited for the due date without reason. He will develop a habit of paying bills on time or avoiding payments altogether, which could lead to serious consequences that will come out of his salary. Not only that, but he misuses payments, which also affect his debt compensation history. Perhaps paying a small proportion of penalties doesn't seem like an awful thing, but doing it too often and his credit score will suffer.

Not saving enough Money

Since we're on the very theme of poor economic money administration, not saving money on a daily basis is by far the most disturbing thing. He doesn't think, what if he loses his job? Or suddenly he will fall ill.

How will he manage to live for some time before he gets back on his feet? There are many other reasons he should start saving cash as well. Saving Money for retirement should be a matter of urgency for him. Putting Money Aside for his next vacation feels like a good strategy too. He should also save for a large purchase, like a new computer or even a dream car. If he has cash, he will not end in debt.

Buying what you want instead of what you need

If you look at his shoes or clothes, you will find that he always has more than he would ever wear. He would be in the habit of exchanging his car for a new one after some years. He will be buying the latest iPhone with your old one still in use. This all sounds familiar as you're talking about a donkey of financial education who hasn't learned anything about saving money and making the right financial decisions for him and his family. There is a need to learn the difference between what you want and what your requirements are. Just think about how much money he will be wasting on new car payments if his old one is still in great form. Or how much money he would save if he won'tbuy a new phone after few months.

Impulse purchasing

Impulse purchases is another habit of the donkey of financial education. He might not feel it right away because it's typically small things he buys impulsively at the start. Maybe he had done shopping once or twice with Money and noticed he bought more items than he originally thought of buying. However, impulse buying might not be so gullible. Narrow sales, unusual offers, or big flashy signs telling how much one would save if he made a purchase right away will be affecting his budget.

Getting into debt

There is no need to explain as it is evident that getting into debt is the foulest way to Save Money. He spends money on lavish clothes, cars as these are his priority and therefore runs short of Money.

Borrowing Money

A donkey of financial education always relies on borrowed money, which means he is not able to manage his own finances smartly. But that doesn't seem good. Whether he is borrowing Money from his nearby ones or he just need a payday loan, he will be considered in debt. And if he couldn't plan on returning the borrowed money, he'll either be emailed by debt collectors, or he'll lose the friendship of people who trusted him enough to provide him with cash. If he needs a quick money fix, he will be trying to rationalize or earn something on the side. Borrowing Money, even for a short time period, is not a good monetary decision.

Being too stingy

If he ever intends to save, the donkey of financial education makes such irrational financial decisions in order to save money. He will buy cheap car fuel from untrustworthy sources and end up rescinding his car engine. He will be buying food that's about to expire just for the reason that it's cheaper and risk getting sick. Saving Money is a good thing, but he should being stingy and selfish, which is a totally different story. He is doing this because he hasn't learned the difference between the correct budget decisions and the ones that could lead to disgusting consequences.

Not learning about money management:

A common mistake that the donkey of financial education makes is to not learn about money management. He might belong to the poor, middle, or upper class. He will be making buying liabilities, which he thinks are assets, just because of lack of awareness and poor performance in the financial education report card. He should know that becoming good with Money is about more than earning to meet your needs. He should never waste his energy in worrying that he isn't a math expert; great calculation skills aren't actually necessary; he just needs to be aware of basic mathematical skills. Life is much relaxed when he will have good financial skills. How he spends his Money creates an impact on his credit score and the extent of debt he ends up carrying. Suppose he is struggling with money management problems like living income to paycheck despite earning more than abundant Money and facing a spending decision, especially a large buying decision. He shouldn't assume he can't afford something. He should remember that just because the money is there doesn't mean he can make the purchase. And for this, he should learn the art of financial management.

The person who gets a C on the financial report card:

He is the person who spends in an irrational way. Although he saves Money, he spends and invests his money with a minimum of logic. His financial performance is weak and relatively; therefore, he gets a 'C' grade and is awarded remarks of unsatisfactory performance. Here are some of the traits of a person with a satisfactory financial report.

Never Following a Budget:

The perpetually poor-performing person never seems to get the art of making financial arrangements. A budget is one's sturdiest tool in order to control his finances. It helps you in determining how much amount one should spend on different items. It empowers you to start saving or to how to pay back the debt. Many people don't like the idea of budgeting or think that things will ultimately work themselves out. But the truth is that everybody (irrespective of how much money they earn) should spend their Money according to a budget. Unless a person does not set limits, he has the capacity to spend more than he can make.

Spends Too Much on Discretionary Purchases

Everyone had a little bit habit of spending money, but the majority of Money of grade 'C' person is spent on unrestricted purchases, and he may find himself becoming perpetually spreading thin fiscally, or even unable to pay his bills. This can include spending too much on privileged items like video games, shoes, or dining out. If he had taken small steps to cut back on this needless spending, he could make a huge difference by setting a goal for himself.

Doesn't Plan for Emergencies

As he is always spending with little logic, he is not prepared for the unavoidable financial emergencies in his life. It has the potential to cause serious financial stumbling blocks. That's why he is in need of an emergency fund. An emergency fund is an account for savings with around six months of active expenses, for the purpose of covering in the case of an unforeseen loss of a job, repair of car, or medical issue. If he had an emergency fund, it would help in preventing him from going further into debt by depending on your credit cards to cover an unpredicted emergency.

Lacking a Clear Financial Plan

People who get a C grade on financial education report card never care to have a vibrant financial plan. It is as you plan to go hiking without a clear chart or route to follow. There is a possibility of ending up seeing some pretty things, but it is very likely that you may get lost and never reach your last stop. In case you have a financial plan, you might not end up following your financial plan perfectly, it will still be helpful in prioritizing your goals. It's like having a map for your financial life that will help in determining the direction you will be going to have for the next step of your plan. A financial adviser provides you help in fine-tuning the plan and determining the best investments to help you influence your goals.

Does Not Set Financial Goals

Budgeting and saving Money are pointless for such type of person as he never has clear goals that he should be working toward. Financial goals and financial organization always go hand-in-hand. These People always seem to be penniless as they neither set goals nor follow through to make them occur. If he has the intention to change his situation, he needs to set rational goals with a perfect timeline. It could be the basic step in getting out of debt or saving up for a paying back on a home.

Spending Money as Soon as They Get It:

These persons have the capability to rush to the store as they receive Money. It seems as Money will make a hole in their pocket. Many people belonging to this category spend the majority of the Money as soon as they get it. This might be because they have the habit to spend paycheck immediately and have feeling that if they run out of groceries, they need to head to the store, or it could be due to pitiable spending habits. However, if he had trained himself to save money by cutting his spending and balance his additional spending, he will be in a much better position money-wise. The key to doing this is through the budget and getting control of your expenditure.

Carries Balances on Credit Card:

People with poor financial record tend to pay interest rather than make others pay it.

They might be near the boundary on their credit cards and, therefore, will carry a balance each month. He will be carrying a balance each month and paying interest, and he will not begin to form wealth. It is vital that he stop using your credit cards and work on getting rid of interest.

Lottery tickets

He is spending with little logic because he believes in the concept of getting rich by lottery. That's why he is burning Money fast, and his rich habits only don't involve a stop at the convenience store on a weekly basis. However, his chance of winning the Powerball grand prize is about one in millions of entries. Those odds could never be in his favor. He should never waste his hard-earned money on chance when he can put it in an investment for use in retirement or college tuition. It can be said that persons with better financial records normally make a more logical choice and invest their money in productive places. You might want to consider doing the same. Many studies have shown that people who might be poor in management of Money play the lottery much more regularly than financially efficient people.

Interest on credit cards

A credit card is similar to eating from a mug of ice cream. You may feel a little guilty for over involving afterward, but it's just too easy. Sure, it's convenient to jab the plastic — but you won't catch affluent people accumulating high credit card interest. They know it will be a waste of money. To avoid accumulating interest, transfer or combine your debt to a credit card with a zero introductory. You should make sure to pay back your balance before the promotional period ends. Another option is to associate any non-deductible debt into a second loan or home equity line of credit, which may be deductible as it depends on your specific condition. Once if you've been out of the red, live on less than you are receiving as salary. "If you can train yourself to spend Money logically and save a considerable amount for your future, you can make Money steadily and not need to depend on credit cards or other non-deductible debt.

Inflated interest rates

Credit scores play an important role in defining your interest rate for loans, loans, and more. Just by having a sophisticated credit score, you can save a huge amount of dollars in interest over the life of a loan. People with second-rate scores, however, might not be able to land loans at all. Financially successful people keep their credit reports clean as they bill on time, keeping debt levels low and fixing blunders on their credit reports. And if you already have a good credit history but you have the habit of carrying a balance on some credit card accounts, consider calling people who issue a credit card to request a higher credit limit. A higher limit will lessen your credit use rate and will ultimately boost your score. When you're on the phone, it won't be wrong to ask for a reduction in rate. If you have lower your interest rate, then you can discharge balances more fastly.

Impulse buys

The person who has not performed well on a financial report card enters into a store intending to purchase one thing but ends up buying more things than which are required. Maybe he won't use that in a while, for instance, buying unnecessary items at the grocery store, so you caught a few extra items. Or perhaps it was a complete sale on your preferred clothing website, and you are fond of buying stylish designer shoes. Whatever the circumstance might be, this isn't a shopping practice for the financially efficient person. Successful people are managers, and impulse buying tends not to mess with this quality. This person needs to emulate this behavior and be much more careful with your Money. One method is to go cash only and not rely on credit-based savings. He should make use of the envelope system so that you bring with you only a prearranged amount of money to use at each store. This approach will help him stay on budget and control any habits he may ordinarily have in impulse buying and overconsumption. Financial guru Warren Buffett describes his own tactic in order to avoid impulsive decisions. He is of the opinion that a person should spend almost a lot of time, almost once a week, in order to just sit and contemplate for more reading and thinking, and making less compulsive decisions, than other people in any business.

Spending on High-end brands

You may have seen a lot of designer labels on the red carpet, but many financially wise people don't pick designer labels for buying items. Though they have the funds to display at luxury retailers, they understand that it will only cost them their hard-earned cash and nothing else. Financially successful people understand the quality of products at the shop and buy the products of both quality and cost. They will go for a cheaper item or purchase the higher value item from a low-priced store in order to make a prudent financial purchase. So my advice to the donkey of financial education is to always shop intelligently and keep your budget and financial objectives in mind.

Investment in Bad real estate

Millennials and financially illiterate people should keep in mind that they should look at property as a multiplier of income rather than as a place to put down roots. The person who gets a C on a financial report card must make wise investment decisions. If a person is investing in real estate, but its value is not increasing, it means that his investment will not yield any result, and his income will remain the same even after investment. The purpose of investment hasn't been fulfilled.

Extravagant inheritances

Financially effective families are time and again in a position to provide the younger generation the help when it comes to expenditures like education and housing.

Many rich and financially efficient persons have publicly announced plans to leave a large sum of money to charitable causes rather than keeping it all in the family. For instance, Bill Gates, who is second the richest person in the world has talked aboutthe plans to contribute a share of his wealth to the Bill and Melinda Gates Foundation rather than giving it to his three children. And Facebook founder Mark Zuckerberg and his wife Priscilla Chan, who have two daughters, have vowed to donate more than ninety percent of their Facebook stocks to generous causes during their periods.

Tons of TV channels and video games

Financially successful people spend considerably less time on video screens of all kinds than their lower-income counterparts. That's especially true when it comes to television and video games. Spending time on screens of all types reduces one's ability to contemplate and focus on serious money matters. He can spend this time more prudently by contacting financially effective people and educating himself about fiscal management issues.

- **Keeping up with the standard**

One of the most financially reckless decisions financially poor educated person makes is trying to meet standards. He is the routine of displaying off with their new car, expensive vacations, the newest Smart TV they just approve of. These are standards too, and he thinks that other people are judging him based on his lifestyle; therefore, he should work on that aspect. However, trying to surpass your neighbors in terms of the standard is definitely a poor financial choice. He should stick to what he can afford and shouldn't feel worried by appearances.

Habits of financially efficient person:

A financially efficient person is someone who earns a considerable amount of money, spends it wisely by making a budget, saves cash for the unfortunate situation, and then invests in a valuable endeavor that increases the value of his Money. In this, he becomes successful in generating a cash flow and never faces a problem of debt or negative income cycle. This is all because of the fact that he has learned the art of financial by performing brilliantly in financial education.

Owing to his outstanding performance, his tutor gives him a grade of 'A+,' which is only given to those students who perform extra-ordinary in this domain.

keeping a Budget:

Financially inefficient persons don't like to budget because they don't want to go through as they consider it a boring process of gathering expenses, adding up numbers, and making sure everything is lining up. If you're not good with money, you shouldn't be excusing with budgeting. In contrast, a financially efficient person keeps track of spending by utilizing a few hours working on making a budget on a monthly basis. You can also do it. Instead of focusing on the process involved in making a budget, focus on the worth that budgeting will convey to your life.

Using the Budget:

The budget is not of any use if a person makes it, then let it gather dust in a folder slipped away in his bookshelf or at someplace cabinet. But a financially efficient person Refer to it often all through the month to help control his spending decisions. He updates it as he pays bills and spends on other expenses of food and grocery items. At any given time during the month, he then gets an idea of how much money he will be able to spend, bearing in mind any expenses he has left to pay.

setting a Limit for Unbudgeted Spending:

A critical part of his budget is the net income or the sum of money left after subtraction of expenses from income. If he has any money left over, he can use it for fun and entertainment, but only up to a specific amount. He never went crazy with this Money, especially if it's not much and it has to last the whole month. Before he makes any big purchases, he makes sure it won't interfere with anything else he has ever planned for the long term.

Tracking Spending:

Small purchases at various places add up quickly, and before you know it, you've already spent much of the income of your budget. Therefore, a financially wise person starts tracking his spending to discover places where he may be naively overspending. He saves receipts and writes his purchases in an expenditure journal, classifying them, so he identifies areas where he has a hard time keeping his spending in check. □

Doesn't Commit to Any New Repeated Monthly Bills:

Just because your revenue and credit qualify you for a definite loan doesn't imply you should get it. Many people ingenuously think the bank won't approve them to get a credit card or loan they can't have the funds for. The bank only knows your profits, as you've reported, and the debt responsibilities included on your credit report, not any other compulsions that could impact your payments and receiving on time. A financially efficient person makes the decision whether a monthly payment is reasonable based on his income and other monthly obligations.

Making Sure he is Paying the Best Prices:

You can make the most of your Money through relatively cheap shopping, ensuring that you're paying the lowest price for products and facilities. He will be looking for discounts, coupons, and cheaper replacements whenever he can.

Save Up for Big Purchases:

The ability to delay satisfaction will get you a long way in helping you be better with Money. When you tend to delay large purchases rather than to give up more important essentials or to place the purchase on a credit card, you are giving yourself time to evaluate whether the purchase is inevitable, and you will have even more time to make the decision on prices. For the purpose of saving up instead of using credit, you are avoiding paying interest on the buying. ☐ And if he is saving rather than skipping bills or obligations, well, he is in a position that he won't deal with the many penalties of missing those bills.

Limiting Credit Card Purchases:

The person who is excellent in money management knows that credit card is the worst enemy of cash or Money. When he runs out of cash, he will not simply return to his credit card without thinking of whether he can afford to get the balance. He will fight the need to use his credit cards for buying when he can't afford them, especially on unnecessary and needless items. □

Contributes to Savings Regularly:

If he deposits Money into a savings account monthly basis, he is aware of the fact that it helps him build healthy business habits. He will set it up, so the Money is spontaneously transferred from his checking account to his savings account. That way, he doesn't have to take the pain to go to the bank and transfer the money into a savings account.

Understands that Being Good with Money demands Practice:

In the beginning, he won't be in the habit to plan like other persons who are donkey of financial education, but there comes a time, when with ample practice, he develops the habit of delaying purchases until he can afford them. The more he makes these behaviors part of his daily life, the more convenient it is for him to manage Money, and the better off his finances will be.

Tricks used for money management in terms of investment by a financially efficient person:

Money management refers to how one takes care of all facets of his finances, which involves budget formation to the movement of money in the account to having long-term goals to choosing investments that will help you reach the goal of valuing your Money. Financially efficient doesn't the meaning of money management as delaying or refusal to any purchase, but developing a plan that gives him the capacity to say yes to the things that are most important to him. Any amount of money can turn to be of little value if he doesn't have excellent money management skills. The start of good money management allows him to know where he is at in terms of assets and obligations. The assets might include bank accounts, investment accounts, saving accounts, and real estate, like housing and car. At the same time, the liabilities include credit card balances, tuition fees, car loans, mortgages, and other debts. It is a general concept that when assets are subtracted from your liabilities, you get your total worth. If your debts are greater than your assets, your net worth is low. But a person with an excellent financial record has changed it, just through efficient money management.

Setting Goals for finance

If you have better goals, you can manage your money more efficiently. The blunder which is committed by the donkey of financial education is that he always overlooks his long-term plans in favor of just trying to find out which bills are getting paid today. However, by setting goals, he can set priority to which expenses are essential and which ones you can delay and wait on. There isn't a universally accepted interpretation of right and wrong when it comes to your expenditure goals, but it takes determination and smart work to attain them. For instance, if he wants to get his dream, which is to have a car that costs $30,000, he has to make more savings than someone who only wants to spend $20,000 on a car.

Managing Multiple Accounts

As he saves for different goals, he will likely have Money in numerous accounts. For instance, for keeping an emergency fund in a discrete savings account, so he isn't tempted to tap it for an instinct purchase. Also, he makes use of an IRA or 401(k) plan to keep his retirement nest egg separate from his other Money. He'll also use different policies for goals with different time possibilities. He might be able to be more hostile investing in stocks and bonds with funds in his retirement account if he won't need the money for nearly three decades. On the other hand, he will want an account without any jeopardy, such as an investments account, for his crisis fund because he could need that cash at any time. There are software programs that help to keep track of numerous accounts to make sure he is staying on track with you're spending and savings goals.

Focus on growing his asset column

Many of us think that financial liberty means amplified income levels, and that is why we often attempt to increase. Even though an increased level of income provides some reprieve in the short-term, in many cases, as one's profits increase, their expenses also increase. This infers that enhancing the income level may not enable him to attain financial autonomy in the long-term. In order to get a long term solution to his fiscal woes, he will focus on building and increasing his asset column of the fiscal statement. When his asset column grows, income mechanically grows. Therefore, the lesson for a financially inefficient person is that his focus should be on Money from the assets that enable him to obtain an income level that is more than his expenses. While many people spend most of their time and energy on making more, it is imperative to take note that without getting to know the art of spending Money well along with sensible saving and prudent investing, they may not be able to produce a hopeful future for themselves and their families.

Money plays an important role in everyone's lives. On one side, it is used to create wealth for future requirements, and on the other, it serves the purpose of transaction in order to satisfy present needs. While financial planning has allowed individuals to come across life goals by judicious management of Money and assets, it can be said that learning to cope with Money wisely may be the first step for getting the bigger goal. Both these areas call for determining the need, competence, and time frame before having started. Managing expenses is all about getting the accurate value for every rupee spent and suitable decisions on the mode of payment, that is, cash, cheque, credit card, or equated monthly installments (EMIs). The two greatly help in meeting our spending needs with ease and comfort.

Budgeting habit of a person with an excellent financial record:

Making a family budget, which includes regular spending and one-time, even unrestricted, expenses, is a way to be not run out of Money and saving enough for goals of life. Another habit associated with a financially efficient person is to have a family budget, which includes both present and past, even discretionary, expenses, is a way to not run out of money. A person with a budget will get control over his capital. He will be in a decent position to accomplish cash flow and pay short-term payments and make plans for other goals. The problem presented by the donkey of financial education is that budget of one person may vary considerably from another person with a parallel cash flow. This is because the budget is a reflection of our habits and aspirations. It is best to modify spending categories based on past understanding and have well-crafted financial goals on a short-term as well as long-term basis. The basic step is to seek advice from a Certified Financial Planner or a CFP practitioner, which is the best way onward and manage your savings for an auspicious future

Methods to Divide EXPENSES:

- Regular and Non-Discretionary Expenses:

Such expenses include grocery, power, fuel, phone, washing, domestic help, eating out, and showbiz expenses. As these are steady and unescapable, you can always put a broad limit so that they do not go out of hand. In addition, making large and inexpensive purchases with friends and relatives may get you good concessions. Ideally, the correct mode for such transactions is Money, debit card, and/or credit card (only for the credit-free period).

- Irregular and Discretionary Expenses:

These include things like spending on furniture and consumer durables, assets like gold, or spending a holiday on a beach. Since these are too costly, one must plan logically. For example, while spending money on furniture, do a kind of price analysis to determine the value and place from where to make a purchase. These days many types of payment options are available, like cash discounts and zero-interest EMIs, among others.

The art of expense management:

Expense management is the art of controlling your expenses. Only in this way will you get the right value for every coin spent, and you will be able to make appropriate decisions on the payment mode. If the seller is offering zero-interest EMIs, a financially bright person will calculate the cost-effectiveness by making an assessment of hidden costs like the processing fee. The accurate way to make such procurements is Money from the scheduled budget, which may be from the investment body. A credit card is used as a mode of payment rather than a source of finance by a financially intelligent person. Instinct buying for luxurious items out of budget on account of the sale, discount, among others is a strictly no by that person. In addition, he also uses his intelligence to decide the landowning cost in terms of the yearly operative rate of interest. He also analyzes if money can be arranged at a lower cost to get the profit of cash discount. While making payment through credit card, he makes sure to pay by the payable date to evade paying high interest. Interest rates on credit cards are much greater than on additional forms of credit. If he does that, credit card debt may deplete his cash resources fast. Therefore, he makes sure to use credit card judiciously; he has sufficient Money to back credit-card expenses. Therefore, he makes use of debit card.

Chapter 4: Lessons for the donkey of financial education to improve his financial record

A donkey of financial always gets an F in the financial report because he is unable to learn the golden rules of money management and unaware of the benefits of financial education. He has considerable lessons to learn from a person who is investing his Money wisely, earning a huge profit, and has always got A+ on the financial report card. Mentioned below are some of the rules for the donkey of financial education to follow.

Getting THE BEST DEAL

Cooperation plays an important role in order to save money and get the best deal. We should not dillydally ask for courtesy products or services. For instance, we can exchange room tariff in case of hotel reservation to ask for free breakfast, lunch, and dinner and airport pick-up and drop. Consumers also have the right to claims reduction on the maximum marketing price printed on products. With the increase of online shopping, we are able to get good deals on the internet. The web allows us to match the prices of various goods and services and pick the best option. Sometimes it will greatly help in getting discounts and gifts as well. For instance, for books, we can visit online websites like an online retailer,

Amazon, which is the bestselling platform that provides these services, and get the finest deal. We can take flats on lease and purchase/sell other assets through the internet and save brokerage, which can be pretty much high. It will minimize expenses to a large extent.

COST-BENEFIT analysis:

A number of reports for the benefits of consumers are available these days at the beginning of thorough scientific analysis and derivation of logical conclusions. However, these cannot be related to every individual. For instance, lowering the actual expenses of petrol running cars cannot be justified if we compute the extraordinary price of diesel cars, although it can be justified that it is because it has to travel large distances. Moreover, diesel cars need more repairs and have a smaller life. Also, their reselling value is much less than that of gasoline vehicles.

LITTLE BIG LUXURIES

There is a difference in terms of accounting perspective between an individual and a company. If the decisions of the company are fixated on growing shareholder value, the individual's planning focuses on realizing his/her life goals. The company has the ability to justify capital expenditure such as plant and machinery through capacity expansion, devaluation benefits, and corporate taxation. However, seen in this context, buying a high-end luxury car cannot be vindicated without sufficient analysis. Similarly, intangible assets can be enhanced in value and accounted for and downgrading claimed on them, but these may not be related and relevant for the individual. Some exemptions to this could be expenditure towards education in several courses and making a purchase of books and journals, among others, which had longstanding benefits. It could be the procurement of Education loans, if possible. Moreover, certain purchases like spending on an old-fashioned car, a portrait, or a traditional piece may come under the purview of wealth management and substitute investments. It is significant that an income should be judiciously allocated between the present and future spending. For the future, one should save and invest wisely as per our risk craving. For the current expenditures, one should maintain the budget well to be able to meet all expenses. Thus, in conclusion, one can say that no more than one-third of one's disposable income should be used for the purpose of servicing debt, and savings should be at least more than half of the net income. Accordingly, the expenses should not surpass more than half of net income in belief.

THE CREDIT CARD ADVANTAGE

> Helps in meeting budget expenses (provided if bills are paid on time)

>Valuable in the tracking of expenses as the lender is sending a monthly statement listing things that you have made spending on

> provides insurance for air travel, full-time car insurance, and extended warranties on certain items bought on the card

>Reclamation of reward points

> There is a free credit period that gives one enough time to pay up

>Respite from carrying cash

>Other rewards like cash-back and frequent-flier. Credit card companies also associate with vendors to offer reductions to a customer

Flipping the thought process when describing your financial skills

The first step in taking control of your finances is to change the thought process around how you perceive things. For instance, instead of considering and thinking that status can only be achieved by spending on expensive items, the first step in financial education for the donkey of financial education is that he should think that he has not yet learned the exact meaning of things and foolishly thinks of spending on unnecessary and needless things of managing my Money. He has to make sure that he is going to resolve this by learning about finance management. It will be a more empowering way to deal with his miserable state of affairs and talk about his condition. For many people in this category, there is also a haunting question which is deeper than just bad with money declaration as they are of the opinion that it is too late and now he can never be good with Money as it has nothing left to save and invest in a productive venture. But this again is a foolish thought as there is nothing one cannot do if he gets determined to achieve it. It is never too late as the thought of too late is just in mind, and if I am candid with such type of people, it is true that you might be a little late, but it is never impossible to keep track of your spending and put your house in order. You can still be a millionaire. What you have to do is to get rid of your donkey financial habits and start saving, no matter how small, but the most important thing is to get started by cutting your spending as much as you can. This is the easiest way available.

Creating an action plan

An action plan doesn't need to be super complex, especially for the starters. Do not get hung up on databases and budgeting apps. First, you need to analyze where your money is going and what are your total expenditures. Ask yourself, of the last paycheck you get, how did you generally spend it but do not beat yourself up over how you spent it because it is now in the past. The basic purpose of this exercise is simply to figure out your habits. Then ask a question to yourself that how do you want your money to spend. You might not be sure at first but manage to save 10% of your money each month and invest 10% of your money every month. If he just is able to do just these two things, the rest of it is probably going to be pretty easy for him. Now, if you're sitting there and thinking that you might not be able to save 10% of your income by cutting your expenses but you probably can. On the investment side of things, for example, make sure you are taking advantage of any 401(k) match that your employer may be offering. If you have access to a match of the employer, then you do not have to make saving and for it, save the full ten percent yourself. When it comes to savings, you have to save some amount. Setting up steady assignments through inspection account into a savings account, so you do not even have to think about it, and you are not desirous of spending that money.

Facing your debt head-on

For most people, the main reason for not getting finances in order is a liability. But you are able to overcome it. People are missing the wood for the trees when they say something like; he really should not have spent that much on the feast, as he says that Feast is not the problem, my friend. Instead, he should talk about the thousands of dollars that he has to pay loan debt you may have or the untiring balance he carries on his credit cards. But not many people in this category want to face the full amount of their debt. He can challenge himself to do just that by actually writing down accurately how much loan you have. The problem is that the people who write them with debt problems are not even aware of the fact that how much they owe. It is threatening. It is nerve-wracking. But it is the first step toward moving out of debt. He should know exactly how much you owe, how much you're paying every month, and what is the exact month that your debt will be paid off. From there, figure out the maximum you can put toward that debt, especially if it contains high-interest rate, such as credit card debt or isolated loans. For a lot of people who have tens of thousands or more of debt, adding an extra hundred dollars a month can cut off the payback period by years. It is never too late to go in that direction. You can change the way you talk about Money and change your spending decisions. And, for this, most importantly, you have to create an action plan on a weekly basis to change your performance with Money. You have to take control of your destiny, and you can do it.

The way you are handling your money on a daily basis is a huge factor in how efficacious you are in making wealth. If you are cautious while making a budget, you can build a large amount of wealth. On the other hand, if your run-through bad money habits, you may end up insolvent and are not able to reach your financial goals. There are multiple behaviors of perpetually broken people. Unfortunately, there is no single and only way to cut spending in order to put you on the path toward monetary liberty. What works for one person when it comes to the reduction of costs and saving more money may not be suitable for you? When you formulate spending and saving policy of your own, make sure you have been able to live by it, and doing so will help you accomplish your financial goals. Some of the ways where you can reduce spending and wind up with more money in your pocket, in your bank account, and your withdrawal account are.

Reduction of Credit Card Spending

If a person who is a donkey of financial education has to pay off his credit card bills in full every month, he has to get rid of interest charges. But that is not an efficient way. Here are some other tactics you can follow to avoid credit card overindulgence. He should stop storing credit card data online. While it is not difficult to make an online purchase when your data is automatically showing up, he can also motivate himself to overspend. He needs to remove that stored information, either in an online account or on an online browser, which has the capacity to reduce the tendency to make incontrollable purchases. For this, waste almost all of your cards as you may need only one credit card in case if there is an unfortunate situation or for findings you know you will be compensating every month. But it is not important that you need to take every one of them with you in your wallet. If he keeps nearly all your cards out of sight, which will be in his desk drawer, it will significantly help keep him out of debt. You should not always stash away your programmed bill, however. Even if you are not making use of a card, you will need to ensure that he keeps paying back a surviving balance. He needs to move towards cash. Ruminate going on a plastic diet for a short time period and making in-store acquisitions with Money instead of credit cards. This will allow him to think more about every purchase and help restrict his overall spending.

Cooking with family

No matter where you are eating, food isn't going to be low-priced. If you spend on food, it reduces the typical income of a household by ten percent, according to recent research. But if you are trying to eat at home rather than at cafeterias, at least some of the time, you might be able to reduce your food expenses by a considerable margin and soon run out of food budget.

To yield even more savings when setting meals at home, consider:

- Creating a meal plan in a week instead of dining out daily and build a grocery-shopping list based on that plan.
- Clip paper or electronic coupons to cut costs on groceries.
- Shop at low-priced grocery stores and stop buying goods from luxury stores.
- Purchase private-label or nonspecific products, which have a habit of being cheaper than brand-name products. Making unpackaged purchases at warehouse stores as

long as you are purchasing what you actually need and will use.

- Shop Around for Insurance

If you shop around for insurance, you can get lower bonuses. The Insurance Information Institution proposes to obtain not more than two quotes for car, proprietors, and leasers insurance. However, keep in mind that the inexpensive coverage might not be the greatest coverage. Other ideas to save money on insurance include:

- Increasing your deductions.
- Get rid of non-compulsory coverage.
- Ask your insurance administrator about discounts. For example, you will not be able to score a deduction if you are driving less than a certain number of miles per year.
- Hustling your strategies. An insurer might create a reduction of your premiums if you purchase at least distinct types of exposure from them, like car insurance and landowners insurance.

Give Thought to Big Purchases

Big-ticket buying can prompt large-time debt. That's why it is vital to think twice before buying large flat-screen TV you are fond of or that new sofa you have been desiring. One of the humblest tactics for accomplishing this is to have a one or two-day break before making the purchase. You can get by without that item. You can put off the purchase until the item goes on a transaction, or you save enough to purchase for it with cash or pay it with the credit card charge instantaneously. You might eventually realize that you are not actually in need of that new TV or sofa. A person who is the donkey of financial education, before deciding to go ahead with a big purchase, should ask these pertinent questions: Would an inexpensive used item will fulfill the purpose? Is the item for sale? If not, when will it be back on sale? Has he looked around for the best contract? There must be another store selling the item (or a better one) at a lower price. Can he afford to buy it? Perhaps he should be saving up money for the item rather than tapping the purchase on a credit card.

Consider using Secondhand Clothes

Secondhand clothes can dress up your closet and decrease your wardrobe costs and costs that add up more than a thousand dollars a year for the average American. You can go for bargains at places like thrift stores, delivery shops, garage sales, yard sales, and digital retailers such as amazon and Sets. If you are not keen on hunting for deals on secondhand clothes, then here are some other tips for trimming your clothing budget:

- Searching for sales. To double up your existing savings, make sure to check out clearance items when online outlets sell clothes at a discount rate. For instance, famous clothing brands offer sales at the end of the season.
- Choosing excellence over price. A fine and good quality article of clothing typically far more than low quality and poorly made piece of

cloth. So even if one ends up purchasing at slightly greater cost, he will still save if it means he won't need to exchange his finds in the near future.

- Ask for a discount if you notice that a shirt is missing a button or needs some work, bargain for a lower price. Sewing on a new brooch is something you can do at home for zero cost.

- And last but not least, always keep stock of out-of-season items. A person with low financial literacy needs to know this as it can possibly use a low-price swimsuit when there is snowfall on the ground, for example.

- Cutting the Cord

Cutting the cord means ending subscription with those entertainment instruments which are traditional and are now replaced by digital streaming sources. There are so many online video watching services like amazon prime and Netflix, and they are available at low-price these days; you might surprise, but canceling your subscription to old-style cable TV for the purpose of cutting costs is a good idea. Your savings might vary, but one evaluation shows that one could pocket more than a hundred dollars a year in exchange for ending cable TV for streaming services. Other related expenses include internet and cellphone service. You have got several tactics at your disposal for decreasing these bills. Here are some of them:

- Call to cancel service of internet. An internet or cellphone service provider may show his intention to strike a deal to keep you as a customer.
- Lower your habit of renting any equipment. Instead of lending out a router and modem from your internet service provider, spend some money to buy your own and save money in the long run.
- Decreasing the speed of your internet. If you do that, it could reduce your monthly bill, and you might not even feel that you are using the internet at a reduced speed.

- Asking about discounts. If you are signing up with a new internet or android service provider, make sure to find out whether any concessions or elevations are available.
- If you shop around, you can switch to another provider who could pare down your monthly bill. Some providers even offer appealing, money-saving incentives such as paying any early dissolution fees your internet provider may charge.
- Review Memberships and Subscriptions

It is easy to forget about the number of your monthly memberships and subscriptions, especially if the mode of payment is automatic. If you are spending a little time raking through your bank or statements of credit card, you may spot connections and subscriptions you rarely use or have now forgotten because you are not using these subscriptions. The few services which people subscribe to and then not follow through are:

- Membership of a gym: A membership can effortlessly add up to hundreds of dollars a year or more, and it will be the money that's just going to waste if a person never attends the gym.
- Digital subscriptions: it has been found that the typical American spends hundreds of dollars on digital subscriptions, which also includes music services and dating apps.
- Subscriptions of magazine and newspapers
- Subscriptions for the purpose of health and beauty products
- Meal-kit delivery services: These services typically cost at least a hundred dollars a week.

You cannot bear the thought of scrutinizing through your bank or credit card statements in order to find memberships and subscriptions that you can dispose of. Some services will do the work for you, and then either cancel them or make negotiations on lower bills (for a fee, of course).

Change to Reusable

Bottled water might be good to drink, but you may be spitting out that water once you start to think about how much it costs in the longer run. The average American spends over a hundred dollars a year on packaged water. If you have a family of four, that could total more than four hundred dollars a year. Instead, start drinking plain or clean tap water from a recyclable bottle or cafeteria instead. The same reason applies if you are going to eat off paper plates, drink from reusable cups or make your coffee with single time use pods. Apart from saving money, switching disposable products with recyclables ones can help save the atmosphere by the use of plastic and, in turn, reducing waste.

The Bottom Line

For a donkey of financial education, there are various methods of spending less, and for him, methods of saving more, which are outlined above, surely are not the only ways to invest, and he needs to put more money into his checking, savings, and retirement accounts. But those strategies and others will give him more benefit if he is creating a household budget and sticking to it so that he can keep track of his spending it the help of strategies. After all, he might not want to squander all of the hard work he has done on spending less and saving more

Chapter5: How worker ends up in debt because of poor financial education and aggressive marketing

We have given here the example of the inadequate financially educated worker, who is considered as a donkey of financial education. He is working for a long time for a stable company that pays regular salaries and is also providing many benefits. He becomes confident of his economic position and, therefore, starts buying goods from status symbols like luxurious accessories like jewelry, watches, using branded clothes, uses latest generation smartphones and laptops at work. His poor financial education is unable to save him from reckless and irrational decision making, and he gets influenced by the marketing of brands to which we all are attracted to some extent. He ends up creating negative debts such as signing a contract for thousands of dollars and that too with interest. He had to spend fifty percent of his salary in the form of installments. In this way, we can say that he is spending his money or item that has no value or will lose value over time. As he is embroiled in an endless cycle of debt, he is not able to save anything for the future and wasting his money on frivolous items. He has no money left to invest in any productive endeavor and, therefore, cannot afford to enhance the value of his money.

Relationship between aggressive marketing and poor financial education:

In the era of Global competition, commoditization, market fragmentation, every brand and the company is trying to get ahead of the other businesses. They have all converged to create an environment requiring companies to create better marketing strategies in order to succeed in the business community. This convergence symbolizes a new age for marketing in the

21st century, which is also named The Age of Advertisement. In this new age of business and marketing, retailers have to change focus from awareness and image to business outcomes in order to gain profit. Marketers are working under the rules set by the finance organization. They use new skills, tools, and perspectives, and finance's help to market their business, which in turn impact the financial education of employees. Employees get attracted due to aggressive marketing techniques employed by major brands. They sell their products through aggressive marketing due to which employees cannot resist and are forced to make bad financial decisions. That's why they are named as the donkey of financial education. A donkey of financial education is a person who doesn't have any sense or wisdom to make efficient financial decisions. He has no long term goals and is lured by attractive marketing of brands and ends up buying their expensive, luxury, and costly items. For instance, a donkey of financial education buys expensive clothes froma designer instead of buying classy clothes from a store. The role of marketing is evident because market familiarizes the product to the consumer, and due to this, the consumer tends to purchase these products, only because it has been portrayed as an attractive and useful product.

The relationship between finance and marketing have been more hostile than cooperative. In order to alter the relationship, marketing is an art to comprehend the mindset of people involved in finance. Basically, finance people calculate risk and believe in making financially savvy decisions. They need marketing to show them that why it is necessary to buy their product and what distinguishes their product from others. It employs the technique of becoming strategic and by being able to tell them that how much money will come back and when. The main focus of finance is on income, expenses, profit, and bondholder value. For most companies, the old adage which says that cash is supreme still reigns. It does not mean that financial people aren't interested in the brand or they have personal animosity with the brand, but it is that they want the ability to connect the image of the brand and trustworthiness to cash flow. It is not merely an accident that there is a strong relationship between cash flow and the responsibilities of marketing. Marketing is liable in order to help the organization obtain and keep lucrative customers and therefore relate its functions directly to cash flow. The more initiatives of marketing address customer lifetime value, improve the rate of product embracing, reducing customer churn, and lower attainment costs, the better the cash flow of the company. It is up to the customers that how they get impacted by the marketing strategies employed by brands and, in turn, impact their cash flow. Marketing employed by businesses and weak or inept financial management can impact employees and the overall operations of an organization in multiple ways. Incompetent managers exist, and they face many challenges concerning staff members and keeping them stirred. In addition, below-average employees may not be able to stabilize their budgets, increase revenues or proficiently perform other crucial tasks; therefore, they have to work extra hours.

Bad financial management has caused employees to permanently suffer from the dilemma of insufficient finances. As a result, they have to work extra hours for compensation for financial losses, the cost is too high in terms of deep stress, and training becomes unreasonable, which can impact the psychological ability of employees to continue operations.

Impact of bad financial education of an employee:

Low savings and working extra time:

Low savings and extra working hours can be a result of bad personal finance management. When an employee spends on frivolous things in an extravagant manner, he will empty his pockets before his next salary, and as he had minimal savings because of poor financial education, he will be forced to work extra hours in the hope that this time, he will earn more and will save or invest in a suitable venture. But his planning fails because he has become a donkey of financial education and spending irrationally is his habit. He will work extra hours, which will disturb his mental health because of work and finance-related stress and fear of not completing the tasks on time. His health will be affected, and he will strive to maintain good health. In addition, poor financial management may also result in a lack of a balance between work duties and personal life or providing working out.

Reduced Employee Productivity:

Due to stress, an employee does not clearly perform up to the performance expectations and follow up with others about their levels of efficiency. It will also be detrimental to the organization as it can experience reduced revenues. When employees join any company, they always receive a performance plan with the criteria for their positions listed. In this scenario, the employee won't be able to make the organization satisfied with his performance. If management does not set performance standards and follow up with reviews, the employee may not motivate himself to work efficiently. Repeatedly evaluating performance might create an impact, but a gathering of expected requirements will also sap productivity. It is an established fact that weekly work performance is an outcome of low productivity, and it is derived from continuous work.

How employers benefit from employee poor financial education:

Because the employee is a donkey of financial education, the employee works extra hours in order to earn more money. Thanks to the donkey behavior of his employee, the entrepreneur will avoid hiring a new human resource because when he has high workloads, he will be able to count on the donkey of the financial education, who is willing to turn over and do somersaults to earn something more. The net profit created by his company will not end up badly wasted on luxury cars, expensive accessories, etc., but will be reinvested in constructive ventures such as in purchasing machinery, improving production processes, enhancing the scope of work of the company, among others. And if not that this profit that company will earn, it will be destined for the purchase of something that will create value over time. Bad management can lead to a decrease in personal profits in two ways: by not managing personnel properly and not balancing the personal budget. When employees are faced with an employer with excellent financial management and financial literacy, they may spend their time looking for his service, and as he is focusing on reaching the long-term goals of the organization, he will take the services of employees in other tasks. He is benefiting from employees in multiple ways. First of all, by not employing others, he has saved his organization from Burdon of excessive human resources. He is taking extra work from that employee, and this employee is suffering from the consequence of his own financial mismanagement. This causes the business to pay an industry wage for high production. Secondly, he is making use of the earned by that employee and investing it in the productive endeavor. So it creates a situation where the company is enhancing its profits on the back of the personal financial inefficiency of an employee.

How employers invest the profit earned due to donkey behavior of employee:

Equity Investments in Small Businesses

The employer could make an equity investment in his business from the profit that he earned through the use of his own financial education. The concept of equity investment is that employer is buying an ownership stake, or it may be like buying a piece of the pie in another business. Equity investors provide only capital, and it is most of the time in the form of cash, in exchange for a proportion of the profits (or loss). The business then makes use of this invested cash for a variety of activities such as capital expenditures needed for the expansion of business, money for carrying out daily operations, decreasing debt, or contracting new employees. In a large number of cases, the fraction of the business the investor receives is relative to the total capital he or she has provided. For instance, if an employer has invested thousand dollars in cash and other investors put in nine thousand dollars, you should expect ten percent of any profits or losses that occur because you provided one-tenth of the equity. In other cases, the proportion of ownership and dividends can fluctuate. Consider the investment partnerships famous entrepreneurs ran at their younger age. For instance, warren buffet had limited partners, and they contributed nearly all of the capital for his partnerships, but profits were split in the ratio of seventy-five to twenty-five. There were limited partners, and he received twenty-five percent in proportion to their complete share of the capital, despite having put up minimum amount of his own money. The limited partners agreed to this preparation because Buffett was providing the know-how about the business to his fellow partners. An equity investment in a small business has the potential to result in the biggest gains, but there are also some of the most risks attached to it. If expenditure becomes higher than sales, part of the losses are also transferred to investors. If it turned into a bad year with massive losses, the company might fail or go insolvent. However, if things go well, returns can be substantial.

The other side: consequences of bad management in business

Bad management is the reason behind permanently closure of doors of organizations. Poor leadership allows high turnover of employees as more employees seek to get benefit; the cost of enrolment and training becomes excessive, which can impact the ability of business to continue operations. Bad management may create an impact on the coffers directly, too, if company finances are mismanaged or the budget is overstretched in comparison with profits earned. Without adequate business reserves, it becomes very difficult and your business not be able to absorb constant losses, and your organization can fail.

Chapter 6: Art of economic frugality

Often the first meaning that enters your mind when you hear the word "frugal" is anybody who is not interested or not like the idea of spending money. Many people attach the word frugal with the punishing cases of people who seldom spend money and make great sacrifices in order to guard their assets.

The Actual meaning of being Frugal

In authenticity, being frugal is to manage your resources and making careful, deliberate buying. This means that a frugal person is very wise in spending his money, but it does not mean that he is not able or willing do the things that he loves the most in a cost-effective manner. It is important to be frugal in a vigorous way that emanates from a positive mindset and related towards money matters. The key to accepting a more frugal lifestyle is identifying the areas where you may need to cut back and selecting the areas where you feel that you have earned the right to display a little bit more remaining within expenses. A prudent person is familiar with the fact that no matter how much he/she wants a certain item, if she is not able to pay cash for it, then she should not have it. She also looks ahead to make an analysis if this particular purchase is going to make it problematic to buy groceries at the end of the month. She has grasped the basic financial skills so that she remains in control of her money and her sentiments when she limits her spending. This is due to her belief in saving in order to achieve higher goals and priorities.

Meaning of Frugal Lifestyle

When you have made a decision to become thriftier it does not mean giving up on everything you enjoy. Rather, it means listing what you enjoy, your financial aims in the context of investment and saving, and deciding which activities you will focus on priority and what will be mislaid. You can have a large amount of optional income, and adore a wide variety of activities while still being economical. You can get a grip on a more frugal lifestyle without fully reducing expenses on everything that you enjoy. The key is that you are working towards explicit financial ambitions while you are enjoying those things. It also means carefully making a research before purchasing and analyzing activities and looking for the best deals on them. Being careful usually means you have mastered the necessary financial skills so that you can begin to make wealth.

Examples of Easy Belt Tightening

For instance, if you are striving to tighten up your budget, but you feel that the basic entertainment channels at cable television are your need for the purpose of relaxing at the end of the day, you can still have both. Cutting back your cable bundle to one where you make use of all of the channels and have limited quality services. Some people may pick to cut cable television entirely and switch to digital video services providers that allow you to still enjoy watching shows. Other actions include diminishing the amount you spend on eating out each month to reimburse within your budget. If you love to travel, you can still have a trip, but you might spend more time looking for the best arrangements for tickets, voyages, and activities. You can also make an effort to find the designer labels you want by shopping at shipment stores to find the items for less money. These examples are a few of the methods you can be more frugal without seriously impeding your overall lifestyle.

Watching Your Spending

The crucial aspect to everything is not to overspend or give in to every indulgence that you crave for. It is important to practice restraint so that you may have control of your assets. If you are spending on an impulse on daily basis, you are not having a frugal lifestyle. You need to make a budget every month and plan for purchases such as new clothes, and entertainment expenses as a part of your consistent budget. Being frugal does not mean giving up and not having your fun, but you should definitely be planning it out before making a trip and making sure that you can truly have the capacity to buy the things you want to do the most. You can also consider finding fun economical activities that you enjoy without spending a large amount of money.

Living within Your Means and Saving for the Future

You could approve of a more frugal lifestyle right now by cherry-picking one thing you want to keep and two things you are eager or enthusiastic to give up in order to do that. As you work to live within your resources and save up for the retirement, you will be able to relax for a while, and really enjoy life without all the financial concern. These things may help you regulate to a pay cut so you can take a less demanding job and improve your worth of life. You should motivate yourself to take a frugal challenge to see how much you can save without cutting out the things you love the most. It will be a huge fun.

Importance of having financial goals:

Whatever it is your aims and ambitions to do in your future, whether work related or other actions, your economic goals in the present should be genuine and reality based so that they may enable you to fulfill your plan. Taking control of your private finances begins when a person thinks about his goals and decides what really matters to him. In this way, he does not indulge in frivolous habits and do not become donkey of financial education. Here are some things to think about which are it is significant for a college student to graduate from college with minimal debt. What are his main aims for summers and other pleasure time? He should work in order to make money and earn for himself. He should take nonpaying internships or volunteer to gain experience in his field. Along with that, he should also enjoy social activities and time with friends. You should ask yourself, what is more important for you, to you to live in a nice place, or drive an expensive car, or wear fine clothes, or eat in wonderful restaurants? What is more important in comparison, your get up or educational goals? There are no convenient answers to such type of questions. Most people would like adequate money to have and do what they want, low enough expenditure that they do not have to work too much to keep track of the budget, and enough financial freedom to pick activities without being influenced by financial concerns. Few students of college or university live in that world, however. Since you always need to make choices, it is important first to think about what actually matters to you and to what extent, you are willing to sacrifice for a while in order to achieve your goals.

The dilemma of Making More or Spending Less:

That often becomes an issue for employee or employer alike. You achieve the goal of setting up a realistic budget and sticking to it. A budget is basically the best way to stabilize the money that comes in with the money that you are spending. For most employees, the only way to increase the money receiving or coming in side of the budget is to start working. Even with financial support from your near ones, financial aid from the financial institution, your savings from past jobs, and the like, you will still need to earn extra money if all your possessions do not equal the cash spent side of the budget. The major theme of this debate is to avoid a debt except when absolutely necessary to finance your needs.

The question is why it has so much importance. Simply because money problems and debt cause more people to go into depression and face mental health problems than any other lone factor. The focus should be on saving more and spending only when required. But working too much can have a negative impact by taking up time you might need for other tasks of life. It's critical, therefore, each time you think about your own financial situation and the need to work, you should also think about how much you need to work and consider whether you would be better-off spending less if that meant you could work less and enjoying your personal life and working more. As we'll see later, employees often spend more than they actually need to and are often more contented and at more advantage once they learn to spend less. Many people get into financial trouble because they are focusing on spending too much not because they are making (or getting) too little. Therefore, the key is to manage finances in an efficient and wise manner.

How to be economically frugal:

The good place to start is that having money or not having money does not define your worth or wellbeing. Your actual friends will think no less of you if you make your own dinner and eat it during free time at job or take the bus to your workplace rather than drive a brand new and luxury car. You are appreciated more by others who matter for you, for who you are as a person, not for what things you have or what is their net worth. You don't have to spend as much as your friends to be considered as wealthy or rich. Some people always have additional money than others because of their family and that is why they always spend more. Fight any feeling that comes to your mind about your friends who are big spenders are the norm and you should follow the suit. You should never feel that you have to go along with whatsoever expensive activities they suggest just so you fit in.

A positive attitude is recipe to success. Learn to stay confident and not get stressed out and anxious about money. If you need to make deviations in how you spend money, view this as an exciting achievement, not a discouraging fact. You should feel good about staying on a budget and being cannyabout how you spend your money. Being realistic about what you can achieve. Most people have financial problems, and they do not just end by waving a magic wand of good intents. The only difference is that they learn the art of solving their problems instead of needlessly worrying about them. If your budget is telling that you do not have enough money even while working and sensibly governing you're spending, you may still need a bank loan or larger alterations in your lifestyle to get by. That is ok as there are ways to deal with that. But if you idealistically set your visions so high about spending less and saving a lot, you may become depressed or disheartened if you are not able to act on your goals. Before making an actual budget, you need to take a look at your purchases and how you are spending money on now and ruminate what is essential and what is not necessary and could be skipped for now because it is optional.

Indispensable costs are due to some big things which are:

- Apartment and board or rent/mortgage, services, and groceries
- College education expenditure like, fees, textbooks, supplies
- Expenses on Transportation
- Insurance like health insurance, car insurance, etc.
- Fee of Dependent care if you need it
- Essential personal items (some sartorial, food, hygiene items, etc.)

These things are occasionally called fixed costs, but that term can be misguiding. If you have the option to move to a less luxurious apartment that is less significant in location or a few blocks farther away, you can easily pay for that and control that cost, so you can say that it is not really fixed. Still, for maximum people, the real savings can be achieved from spending less on non-compulsory things. Most people spend out of habit, not really discerning about where their money goes or how quickly their spending is increasing. If you knew you are spending more than a hundred dollars a month on coffee you buy every day between work hours, you will think twice before having a coffee. Or another thousand on fast food dinners although it only takes a couple minutes in the morning to make your dinner? When people will actually start paying attention to where their money is going, most are shocking to see how their totals grow. If you can save less than thousand dollars a year by cutting back on just the little items, it will go too far in order to make you feel much better about your financial situation.

Some general principles in order to be financially frugal:

Following are some wide-ranging principles for the purpose of learning to spend less.

Being aware of what you are spending.

You can Carry a small notepad and write down everything and daily routine of how you spend for a month. You'll see your conducts and you will motivate yourself to be able to make a better budget to take control of your spending.

Looking for substitutes.

If you are buying a lot of bottled water, for example, you may feel yourself to be healthier than people who developed the habit of drinking soft drinks or coffee, but you might be spending hundreds of dollars a year on something that is virtually free for everyone else. You should Carry your own reusable water bottle and save the money.

Planning ahead to avoid impulse spending.

If you have a food item in your backpack, it will be much easier for you to not put a dollar in a marketing machine when you are hungry on the way to office. You make include it in your habit to make a list before going for grocery shopping and sticking to it. If you are shopping without a list, there is probability that you will end up buying all sorts of unneeded (and expensive) things that catch your eye in the store. You should be smart and Shop around in order to compare prices, and buy in wholesale. If you just stop for a moment to think before making a purchase, you will save yourself from buying unnecessary items and often, this is all it takes.

How to Manage a Budget?

Budget formation includes analysis of your income and expenditure so you can see which things you are spending your money on and making adjustments when needed to avoid liability. At first budgeting can appear as complicated or overwhelming, but once you have well versed with the basics, you'll find it easy and a very prized tool for adjusting your personal finances. The question arises that why we should create and manage a budget. Going to office might changes your financial situation but there are many new expenses, and you likely not be aware of them until your manage spending needs and analyze habits over the long term. If you do not have a budget, a financially bad person will still be spending more than he has coming in, as evidenced by the fact that most American citizens today are in debt and have to pay mortgage or bank loan. Debt is a major reason many employees work overtime. So it becomes a necessity for that person to go to the worry to create and manage a budget.

Managing a budget includes various steps which are:

- List all your sources of income on a monthly after month.
- Calculate all your expenses after a month and make amendments.
- Make adjustments in your budget and routine if needed to make sure that the money isn't going out quicker than it is coming in.
- Balance Your Budget by reducing irrelevant expenses
- The most important step is to compare your total monthly incoming with your total monthly outgoing and then evaluate total expenses.

For frugal spending, you need to evaluate that your budget is balanced at this point. Remembering that you assessed some of your disbursements and costs. You could not know for sure until you might be able to take note of your expenses for at least a month and have real statistics to work with. You have to find out what will you do if your spending total is higher than your income total. The first phase is to write your whole budget work on paper. If you take not of items in your expenditure list and see where you can make a cut. For instance, employees should not try to live like business owners and employers. You might be used to taking a nice cut and blow every month or two but maybe you can visit a cheaper place for this purpose or cut it yourself. There are a number of ways to spend less, as recommended earlier.

The essential first step is to make your budget stable in terms of income and expenditure on paper. Then your job is to act according to the budget. It is standard to have to make alterations at first. But always keep in mind that you have to keep the overall budget balanced as you make modifications. For example, if you find you are spending more on textbooks, you may choose that you will be spending less on eating out and deduct the amount from that set that you make an addition to the textbook category. You have to get in to the habit of thinking this way instead of going for a credit card when you won't have sufficient in your budget for anything you want or need. You should not be surprised as it will take several months to make the budget process and changing personal habits related to the use of money. You should be flexible, but stay dedicated to the process and never think of giving up because it will feel like to too much work to keep your money on a pathway. If you do not have a budget, you might have a difficulty reaching your ultimate goal which is taking control of your life while working in any position.

What If Your Budget is not working?

Your budget might be unbalanced by a trivial amount that you can correct by decreasing spending, or your budget may suffer from serious imbalance. If your best exertions are unable to cut your expenditures to equalize your income, you might have a more thoughtful problem, unless you are planning in advance to manage this with bank loans or other assets. First, think about how this condition transpired. When you decided to go to office, the main question is how you plan to finance your salary. If you are enthused to reach your business goal, it is good. Now look closely at your budget to decide what is required. If you are unable to solve the budget shortfall by cutting back on extraordinary expenses, then you need more theatrical changes. You need to determine whether you are paying a high rent because your apartment is spacious or near office. If you can move a little farther away and change to temporarily in a smaller place and if the difference in rent makes a big transformation in your overall savings. If you are spending a lot on your car, you can sell it and get by with public transportation for some years until you stabilize your expenses. Learn to play with the numbers for such items in your budget and see how you can cut expenditures to meet your needs without getting genuinely in debt. If you worry you will not be as happy if you make a change in your lifestyle, recall that money problems are a key cause of stress for many employees and employers and that stress will create an impact on your happiness as well as your performance. It is much fruitful if you to work on your budget and prevent this stress. If everything fails, then seek the optional of financial in order to cut back on your expenses. You should not wait until you are in real financial woe before talking to someone who may in a position to offer help.

What If you are in Financial Trouble?

People often do not acknowledge themselves that they have a problem until it becomes uncontrollable and insurmountable. We human beings are good when it comes to giving good reason to cause of problem and making excuses to ourselves. Here are some cautionary signs if you slide into financial trouble: For several months in a row, your budget is disturbed because you are spending more than your income is. You have started using your savings for predictable expenses you think you should be able to handle with your regular budget.

You have skipped a deadline for a bill or are forced to take credit card cash loans or overdrawing your checking account. You have a large amount of balance on your credit card and have paid only the required lowest payment for the last one month. You have zero amount in the bank in case, a disaster arrives. You do not even have any about total amount of total debt owe to creditors. You are trying to cut expenditures by reducing the desire for something important, such as dropping health assurance or not buying required favorite food. If you have experienced any of these warning signs, first recognize the problem and admit it. Obviously, it is not going to solve itself but you need to take energetic steps before it gets poorer and affects your personal and professional life. Second, if you just cannot budget your sense of balance, acknowledge that you need help. There's no shame in that. Start with the financial help office where you can find help, they will educate you in financial domain and help you ride off the donkey climb and help you better manage your finances, so that you do not enter negative income cycle.

The bottom line:

If you are facing problems just getting on with your budget, it may seem useless to even think about saving for the retirement. Still, if you can put aside some amount of cash every month into a savings plan, it is very much valuable effort as an emergency or unanticipated situation may occur anytime. If you have the savings to cope with it is much less worrying than having to find an advance or running up your credit cards. Saving is a good thing to adopt and you should develop this habit. Some frugal financial managers give tips for living a frugal life and they tell you to do things like dispersing the plies on your toilet paper for the purpose of saving a few pennies. But you can learn how to be frugal by reducing expenses on things that do not add meaning to your life, instead of spending hours trying to make reductions in small expenses. Being frugal in most areas of your life stereotypically means you can afford to orgy every once and again, and it can be taken as one of my favorite things about being frugal as it gives one the freedom to enjoy something permissive without any culpability.

Conclusion

Finally, this e-book has been successful in attracting the attention of readers in terms of elaborating the main concepts of financial education and why financial education is important, how person can get the idea of financial education. This section mainly focuses on need of financial learning and how financial literacy can be regarded as the stepping stone for financial education. In second chapter, the concept of money management has been described. It also tells readers about the elements of money management such as budget formation, using credit card and making creative and useful investments. It also explains golden rules of money management which are imperative for making minimal expenditures.

Other section of the book deals with the financial report card of three type of persons. First belongs to the category of person that is very poor in handling finance and therefore termed as donkey of financial education. He is not aware of the art of spending wisely and thriftily, saving for retirement or unfortunate situation and investing in a prudent manner. He has been given the poor grades in his financial report card in the same way as student with poor academic record given F grade. Second type of person is that which earns handsome amount of money but he has habit of spending in illogical manner and therefore is unable to save much. He has been given the grade C in his financial report card as his financial education level is unsatisfactory to grant him good remarks. Third type of person spends efficiently and in wise manner. He is excellent in every domain of financial education such as spending, saving and investing. That's why he gets A+ grade in financial report card.

Next chapter of book deals with consequences resulting from bad financial education of employee. That employee is donkey of financial education as he is making reckless financial decisions by spending on luxurious items and wastes his whole salary and still ends up in debt. This e-book also discusses how his financially savvy employee takes advantage of donkey behavior of his employee and in turn, takes extra work from this employee and invests the saved revenue in a profitable venture. Then last chapter of the book discusses the art of frugal spending and how a person can change his decisions by following the principles of frugal management of finance.

www.ingramcontent.com/pod-product-compliance
Lightning Source LLC
Chambersburg PA
CBHW070352220526
45467CB00001B/355